Israel

DISCOVER ISRAEL CULTURE, SPORTS, HISTORY, CUISINE, LANDMARKS, PEOPLE, TRADITIONS,AND MANY MORE FOR KIDS

LOCATION

North - Lebanon

West - Mediterranean Sea

East- Bordering Jordan

South - Egypt

POPULATION

9.5 Million

China population
1425 Million

India Population
1428 Million

INDEPENDENCE

May 14, 1948

From
British

CLIMATE

Predominantly Mediterranean

Wet season

Dry season

December through February

June through September

CAPITAL

Jerusalem

- Home to important religious sites like the Western Wall.

- Israel's government is based here.

- A city of great historical importance.

- Cultural hub with museums and festivals.

- Unique blend of ancient and modern architecture.

CURRENCY

New Israeli Shekel (NIS)

Denominations notes

20, 50, 100, 200 shekels

Coins - 10 agorot, ½, 1, 2, 5, 10 shekels

EDUCATION

Compulsory from ages 3 to 18, Strong emphasis on technology and science, Recognized for high educational standards and innovation.

LANGUAGE

Official Language

שָׁלוֹם

HEBREW

NATIONAL FLAG

- They are the traditional colors of the Jewish prayer shawl, the Tallit.

- Blue and white also represent the values of purity, peace, and divine revelation.

- The Star of David, is a widely recognized symbol of Jewish identity and Judaism.

NATIONAL ANIMAL

Israeli Gazelle

- Its known for its agility and speed.

- It commonly found in the Israeli countryside.

- It grazes on grasses and leaves.

- It lives in herds for protection.

- It's the important symbol in local folklore.

NATIONAL BIRD

Hoopoe

- Its recognizable by its distinctive crown of feathers.

- It eats insects, making it a natural pest controller.

- It nests in tree cavities.

- It found across various habitats in Israel.

- It's a migratory bird, traveling as far as Africa.

NATIONAL TREE

Olive Tree

- It symbolizes peace and wisdom.

- Its olives are a staple in Israeli cuisine.

- It can live for thousands of years.

- Its important in religious traditions.

- Its olive branches are often used as a peace symbol.

TRADITIONAL MEDICINE

1) Chamomile

- Used to treating insomnia, anxiety, and to soothe stomach ailments and menstrual cramps.

2) Licorice

- Used to treat stomach ulcers and can help with upper respiratory problems.

3) Aloe Vera

- Used for its soothing properties, sunburns, skin hydration, and as a natural remedy for digestive issues.

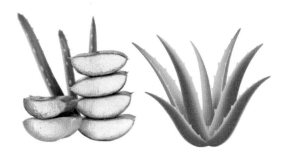

4) Olive Leaf

- Used to help lower blood pressure and cholesterol levels.

NATIONAL FLOWER

Cyclamen

- It blooms in winter, bringing color to the landscape.

- Its flowers range from white to pink and red.

- It grows in rocky areas and woodlands.

- A favorite in Israeli gardens.

- It represents enduring love and beauty.

BEAUTIFUL BEACHES

There are 137 beaches in Israel

Gordon Beach

Banana Beach

Dor Habonim Beach

Frishman Beach

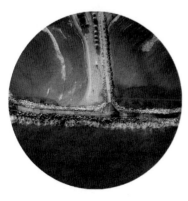

Achziv Beach

Palmachim Beach

NATIONAL PARK

There are 81 National parks in Israel

| Masada National Park | Caesarea National Park | Ein Gedi National Park |

| Yarkon National Park | Avdat National Park | Ashkelon National Park |

LAND MARKS

Timna Park

Mount of Olives

Mount Hermon

Herodium

Rosh Hanikra

Qumran Caves

LAND MARKS

Western Wall

Dome of the Rock

Masada

The Dead Sea

Bahá'í Gardens

Tel Aviv Promenade

ECONOMY
Based on

Tourism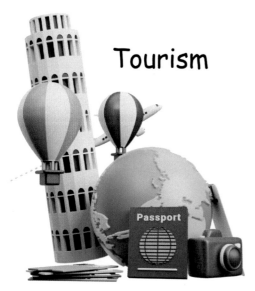

Agriculture

Technology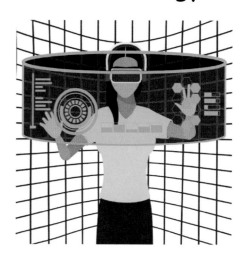

Manufacturing

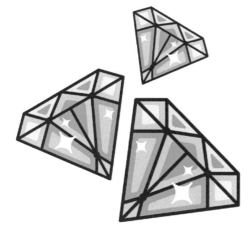

Diamond Export

EXPORTS

Cut Diamonds

High-tech Equipment and Gadgets

Chemicals

Agricultural Products (Citrus, Vegetables)

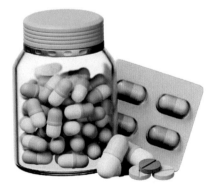

Pharmaceuticals

MARINE LIFE

Eco system most diverse in the world

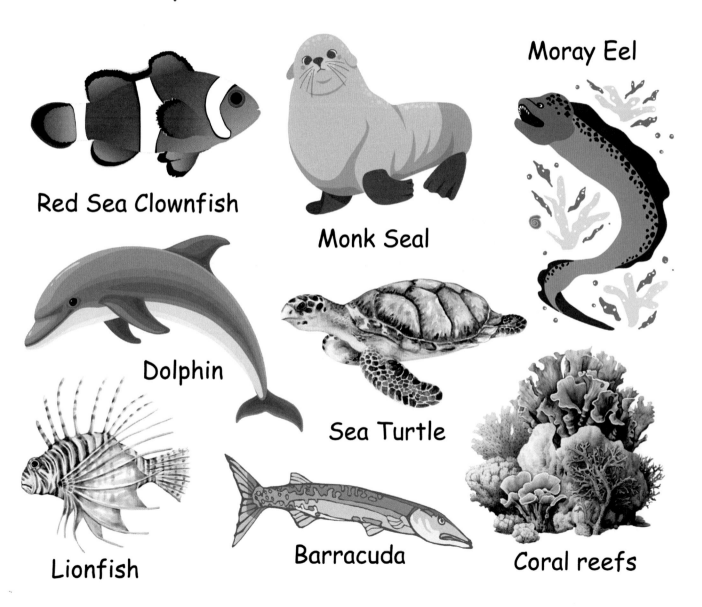

Red Sea Clownfish

Monk Seal

Moray Eel

Dolphin

Sea Turtle

Lionfish

Barracuda

Coral reefs

WILD LIFE

Eco system most diverse in the world

Israeli Gazelle

Golden Jackal

Nubian Ibex

Eurasian Lynx

Arabian Leopard

Striped Hyena

BIRDS & BUTTERFLY

Paradise for birds watchers

591 Species

141
Butterfly
varierty

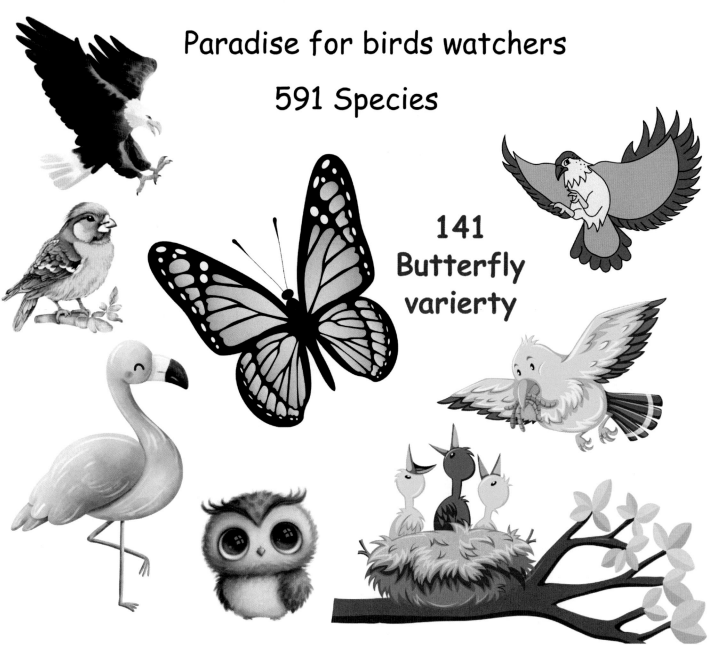

SPORTS & ADVENTURES

Popular Sports are as follows

Soccer

Hiking

Scuba diving

Windsurfing

Basketball

FAMOUS PEOPLE

Golda Meir
(Fourth Prime Minister)

Yitzhak Rabin
(Prime Minister)

Shimon Peres
(President)

David Ben-Gurion
(First Prime Minister)

Gal Gadot
(Actress)

ARTS & CRAFTS

Ceramics and Pottery

Judaica

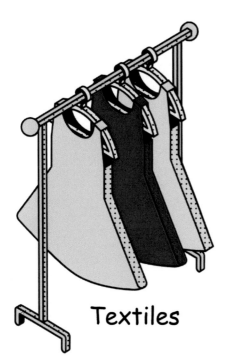

Textiles

Wood
carvings

Handmade
Jewelry

CUISINE

Country has multi cultural society

Hummus

Falafel

Shawarma

Pita Bread

Halva

Latkes

Baba Ganoush

Shakshuka
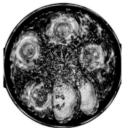

Sufganiyah

Israeli Salad
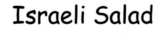

Burekas

FESTIVALS

Passover

Sukkot

Hanukkah

Purim

Yom Ha'atzmaut

MUSIC INSTRUMENTS

Oud

Shofar

Lyre

Kanun

Darbuka

UNESCO- WORLD HERITAGE SITES

There are 16 UNESCO sites in Israel

Masada

White City of Tel Aviv

Biblical Tels

Caves of Maresha

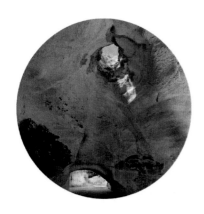

Desert Cities in the Negev

Old City of Jerusalem

INTERNATIONAL RELATIONS

- Israel maintains a complex web of diplomatic relationships, with strategic alliances primarily in technology, defense, and trade.

- It has peace treaties with several neighboring Arab countries, but also faces ongoing conflict situations.

FUN FACTS

- Tiny but Mighty

- Israel is a small country, about the size of New Jersey, but it's packed with history and innovation.

- City of Gold

- Jerusalem is known as the "City of Gold" because of the golden limestone used in many of its buildings.

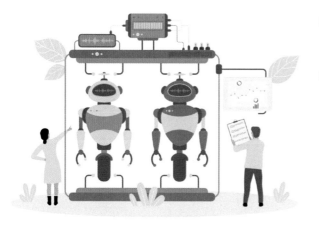

- High-Tech Hub

- Israel is one of the world's leading countries in technology and innovation, often called the "Start-Up Nation."

- Salty Sea

- The Dead Sea is so salty that people can easily float on its surface.

- World's Oldest City

- Jericho, located in Israel, is one of the oldest inhabited cities in the world.

- Lighting Up

- A town in Israel uses solar power to generate all its energy needs during the day.

- Honeybee Species
- Israel is home to a unique species of bee found nowhere else in the world.

- Treetop Walk

- Israel has a place where you can walk among the treetops on a specially designed pathway.

- Kids' Parliament

- Israel has a special parliament just for kids to share ideas on how to improve the country.

- Underwater Museum

- You can go snorkeling over an ancient submerged port town in Caesarea.

- Comic Book Heroes

- An Israeli company helped animate some famous American cartoons and superhero shows.

- Record-breaking Dessert

- The world's largest plate of hummus was made in Israel and weighed over 4 tons.

- Coral Protection

- The Red Sea near Eilat is known for its beautiful coral reef, which is carefully protected.

- Clever Cows

- Israeli cows produce more milk per cow than almost any other country in the world.

Made in United States
Orlando, FL
19 December 2024

56263066R00024